Quoof

PAUL MULDOON

Quoof

Wake Forest University Press

Published in Great Britain
by Faber and Faber, 1983.
Published in the U.S.A.
by Wake Forest University Press, 1983.
Printed in the U.S.A. by
Thomson-Shore, Inc.
Cover design by Richard Murdoch.

ISBN 0-916390-19-5 LC 83-050028

for Ciarán Carson

Wake Forest University Press
Winston-Salem, North Carolina 27109

Contents

But the old foster-mother was a great shaman and, when they had been left alone, and all her neighbours had gone their way, she turned herself into the form of a man and married her adoptive daughter. With a willow branch she made herself a penis so that she might be like a man, but her own genitals she took out and made magic over them and turned them into wood, she made them big and made a sledge of them. Then she wanted a dog, and that she made out of a lump of snow she had used for wiping her end; it became a white dog with a black head; it became white because the snow was white, but it got the black head because there was shit on one end of the lump of snow. Such a great shaman was she that she herself became a man, she made a sledge and a dog for hunting at the breathing-holes.

Rasmussen, *The Netsilik Eskimos*

Acknowledgements

Acknowledgements are due to the editors of *Aquarius, Belfast Review, Buff, Chicago Review, Concerning Poetry, DAM* (Holland), *Digraphe* (France), *Fortnight, Honest Ulsterman, Listener, Literary Review, London Review of Books, New Irish Writing, New Statesman, New World Journal, Observer, The Penguin Book of Contemporary British Poetry, Pequod, Poetry Review, The Times Literary Supplement*, also to the BBC and RTE.

'Trance' and 'Yggdrasill' were published in a limited edition by the Gallery Press (Dublin) and the Deerfield Press (Massachusetts), and several of these poems are included on the Faber Poetry Cassette *Ted Hughes and Paul Muldoon.*

Gathering Mushrooms

The rain comes flapping through the yard
like a tablecloth that she hand-embroidered.
My mother has left it on the line.
It is sodden with rain.
The mushroom shed is windowless, wide,
its high-stacked wooden trays
hosed down with formaldehyde.
And my father has opened the Gates of Troy
to that first load of horse manure.
Barley straw. Gypsum. Dried blood. Ammonia.
Wagon after wagon
blusters in, a self-renewing gold-black dragon
we push to the back of the mind.
We have taken our pitchforks to the wind.

All brought back to me that September evening
fifteen years on. The pair of us
tripping through Barnett's fair demesne
like girls in long dresses
after a hail-storm.
We might have been thinking of the fire-bomb
that sent Malone House sky-high
and its priceless collection of linen
sky-high.
We might have wept with Elizabeth McCrum.
We were thinking only of psilocybin.
You sang of the maid you met on the dewy grass—
And she stooped so low gave me to know
it was mushrooms she was gathering O.

He'll be wearing that same old donkey-jacket
and the sawn-off waders.
He carries a knife, two punnets, a bucket.
He reaches far into his own shadow.
We'll have taken him unawares
and stand behind him, slightly to one side.
He is one of those ancient warriors
before the rising tide.
He'll glance back from under his peaked cap
without breaking rhythm:
his coaxing a mushroom—a flat or a cup—
the nick against his right thumb;
the bucket then, the punnet to left or right,
and so on and so forth till kingdom come.

We followed the overgrown tow-path by the Lagan.
The sunset would deepen through cinnamon
to aubergine,
the wood-pigeon's concerto for oboe and strings,
allegro, blowing your mind.
And you were suddenly out of my ken, hurtling
towards the ever-receding ground,
into the maw
of a shimmering green-gold dragon.
You discovered yourself in some outbuilding
with your long-lost companion, me,
though my head had grown into the head of a horse
that shook its dirty-fair mane
and spoke this verse:

Come back to us. However cold and raw, your feet
were always meant
to negotiate terms with bare cement.
Beyond this concrete wall is a wall of concrete
and barbed wire. Your only hope
is to come back. If sing you must, let your song
tell of treading your own dung,
let straw and dung give a spring to your step.
If we never live to see the day we leap
into our true domain,
lie down with us now and wrap
yourself in the soiled grey blanket of Irish rain
that will, one day, bleach itself white.
Lie down with us and wait.

Trance

My mother opens the scullery door
on Christmas Eve, 1954,
to empty the dregs
of the tea-pot on the snowy flags.
A wind out of Siberia
carries such voices as will carry
through to the kitchen—

Someone mutters a flame from lichen
and eats the red-and-white Fly Agaric
while the others hunker in the dark,
taking it in turn
to drink his mind-expanding urine.
One by one their reindeer
nuzzle in.

My mother slams the door
on her star-cluster of dregs
and packs me off to bed.
At 2 a.m. I will clamber downstairs
to glimpse the red-and-white
up the chimney, my new rocking-horse
as yet unsteady on its legs.

The Right Arm

I was three-ish
when I plunged my arm into the sweet-jar
for the last bit of clove-rock.

We kept a shop in Eglish
that sold bread, milk, butter, cheese,
bacon and eggs,
Andrews Liver Salts,
and, until now, clove-rock.

I would give my right arm to have known then
how Eglish was itself wedged between
ecclesia and *église*.

The Eglish sky was its own stained-glass vault
and my right arm was sleeved in glass
that has yet to shatter.

The Mirror

in memory of my father

I

He was no longer my father
but I was still his son;
I would get to grips with that cold paradox,
the remote figure in his Sunday best
who was buried the next day.

A great day for tears, snifters of sherry,
whiskey, beef sandwiches, tea.
An old mate of his was recounting
their day excursion
to Youghal in the Thirties,
how he was his first partner
on the Cork/Skibbereen route
in the late Forties.
There was a splay of Mass cards
on the sitting-room mantelpiece
which formed a crescent round a glass vase,
his retirement present from C.I.E.

II

I didn't realize till two days later
it was the mirror took his breath away.

The monstrous old Victorian mirror
with the ornate gilt frame
we had found in the three-storey house
when we moved in from the country.

[12]

I was afraid that it would sneak
down from the wall and swallow me up
in one gulp in the middle of the night.

While he was decorating the bedroom
he had taken down the mirror
without asking for help;
soon he turned the colour of terracotta
and his heart broke that night.

III

There was nothing for it
but to set about finishing the job,
papering over the cracks,
painting the high window,
stripping the door, like the door of a crypt.
When I took hold of the mirror
I had a fright. I imagined him breathing through it.
I heard him say in a reassuring whisper:
I'll give you a hand, here.

And we lifted the mirror back in position
above the fireplace,
my father holding it steady
while I drove home
the two nails.

from the Irish of Michael Davitt

The Hands

To the chopping-block, on which the farmer Sebastian split
logs against the Asturian cold,
the Guardia Civil would shove him and spit:
Now clench the fist with which you made so bold.

Four of them held him under.
He writhed and whimpered, in a state of shock.
The axe would fall, and sunder
the hands that had quarried rock.

With bloody stumps he loped across the land.
They laughed as they shot after him. And when he blared
one came over to stop his mouth with loam.

He lay dead in the field. But his far-fetched hands
would stir at night, and the villagers heard
the fists come blattering on their windows, looking for
                                        home.

after the German of Erich Arendt

The Sightseers

My father and mother, my brother and sister
and I, with uncle Pat, our dour best-loved uncle,
had set out that Sunday afternoon in July
in his broken-down Ford

not to visit some graveyard—one died of shingles,
one of fever, another's knees turned to jelly—
but the brand-new roundabout at Ballygawley,
the first in mid-Ulster.

Uncle Pat was telling us how the B-Specials
had stopped him one night somewhere near Ballygawley
and smashed his bicycle

and made him sing the Sash and curse the Pope of Rome.
They held a pistol so hard against his forehead
there was still the mark of an O when he got home.

My Father and I and Billy Two Rivers

Our favoured wrestler, the Mohawk Indian.

We would sit in the local barber shop—
'Could he not afford a decent haircut?'—
to watch him suffer the slings and arrows
of a giant Negro who fought dirty.

The Negro's breath-taking crotch-hold and slam
left all of us out for a count of ten.

The barber knew the whole thing was a sham.

Next week would see Billy back on his feet
for one of his withering Tomahawk Chops
to a Britisher's craw,

                        dusting him out
of the ring and into the wide-mouthed crowd
like a bale of tea at the Boston Tea Party.

Quoof

works as mode of exclusion

How often have I carried our family word
for the hot water bottle
to a strange bed,
as my father would juggle a red-hot half-brick
in an old sock
to his childhood settle.
I have taken it into so many lovely heads
or laid it between us like a sword.

An hotel room in New York City
with a girl who spoke hardly any English,
my hand on her breast
like the smouldering one-off spoor of the yeti
or some other shy beast
that has yet to enter the language.

child context

out of browse

A
B
C
D
D
B
C
A

E
F
G
E
G
F

permutation of enigma

trail/track

- no verb
- foreign, out of context
- exploded, irregular Petrarchan sonnet
- transformative nature of language
- category confusions (plant/mythical animal/human)

distance in sp;
foreign; out of place
punctulum

[17]

Big Foot

Comes, if he comes at all, among sumach
and birches, stops half-
way across the clearing . . . Wood-smoke,
the cabin where you mourn your wife,

where, darkening the tiny window,
is the fur coat
you promised her when she was twenty
or twenty-one, you forget.

Beaver

Let yourself in by the leaf-yellow door.
Go right up the stairs.

Along the way you may stumble upon
one girl in a dress

of flour-bag white, the turkey-red
of another's apron.

Give it no more thought
than you would a tree felled across a stream

in the Ozarks or the Adirondacks.
Step over her as you would across

a beaver dam.
And try to follow that stream back

to the top of the stairs,
to your new room with its leaf-yellow floor.

*a drawing please
to women of
"beaver dam"*

[19]

Mary Farl Powers *Pink Spotted Torso*

I

She turns from the sink
potato in hand. A Kerr's Pink,
its water-dark
port-wine birthmark
that will answer her knife
with a hieroglyph.

II

The open book of Minnesota
falls open at Main Street, an almost total
sky, sweet nothings in the Soda
Fountain, joy-
rides among the tidal
wheat-fields, midnight swims with the Baumgartner boy.

You saw through that flooded granite quarry
to the wreckage of an Oldsmobile,
saw, never more clearly,
him unmanacle
himself from buckled steel, from the weight of symbol,
only to be fettered by an ankle.

[20]

Edward Kienholz *The State Hospital*

Where a naked man, asleep, is strapped
to the lower bunk of a bed.
The bed-pan is so tantalizingly out of reach
we may assume he has trouble
with his bowels.
He will have been beaten by an orderly,
a bar of soap wrapped
in a towel.

His head, when we come to examine the head
we would never allow ourselves to touch,
is a fish bowl
in which two black fish, or mauve,
take it in turns to make eyes and mouths
or grapple with one bright idea.

Yet the neon-lit, plastic dream-bubble
he borrowed from a comic strip—
and which you and I might stretch
to include Hope, Idaho—
here takes in only the upper bunk of the bed
where a naked man, asleep, is strapped.

Glanders

When you happened to sprain your wrist or ankle
you made your way to the local shaman,
if 'shaman' is the word for Larry Toal,
who was so at ease with himself, so tranquil,

a cloud of smoke would graze on his thatch
like the cow in the cautionary tale,
while a tether of smoke curled down his chimney
and the end of the tether was attached

to Larry's ankle or to Larry's wrist.
He would conjure up a poultice of soot and spit
and flannel-talk, how he had a soft spot

for the mud of Flanders,
how he came within that of the cure for glanders
from a Suffolkman who suddenly went west.

The Salmon of Knowledge

Out of the world of blood and snatters,
the inch-tŏ-the-mile

world of the eel,
the yardstick of lymph,

the unquenchable oomph
of her whip, her thigh-length boot

on the other foot,
her hackled gulp of semen—

out of this world is the first salmon
of the year, his ass hole

clean as a whistle.
Here lies one who reached for the sky.

There is a bay-leaf over his eye
and his name is writ in water.

[23]

(handwritten annotations:)
also, pure H$_2$O (woman)
subterranean
world in world
double meaning
(man)
crown of laurels on poets
evaporative/ephemeral yet affecting
over Keats grave
√ knowledge from surprising sources
√ salmon is mythic in Ireland
√ little creation w/ violence/destruction
√ woven as domesatry

From Strength to Strength

A Charolais, the new cow-calf
will plunge out of her own shadow
as if from the bath.

Her bath towel
is a rich brocade.
She pummels herself. A talcum-rime.

She wants to meet the full-length
mirror head-on.
She is palmed off by the meadow,

me, my aluminium bucket.
She takes her milk like medicine.
Though she may lift her fraying tail

to skitter-dung,
she goes from strength to strength,
a grasping, veal-pale tongue.

Cherish the Ladies

In this, my last poem about my father,
there may be time enough
for him to fill their drinking-trough
and run his eye over

his three mooley heifers.
Such a well-worn path,
I know, from here to the galvanized bath.
I know, too, you would rather

I saw behind the hedge to where the pride
of the herd, though not an Irish
bull, would cherish
the ladies with his electric cattle-prod.

As it is, in my last poem about my father
he opens the stand-pipe
and the water scurries along the hose
till it's curled

in the bath. One heifer
may look up
and make a mental note, then put her nose
back to the salt-lick of the world.

Yggdrasill — *N. mythic Tree of Life*

From below, the waist-thick pine
seemed to arch
its back. It is a birch,
perhaps. At any rate, I could discern
a slight curvature of the spine.

They were gathered in knots
to watch me go.
A pony fouled the hard-packed snow
with her glib cairn,
someone opened a can of apricots.

As I climb
my nose is pressed to the bark.
The mark
of a cigarette burn
from your last night with him.

A snapshot of you and your sister
walking straight
through 1958,
The Works of Laurence Sterne
your only aid to posture.

The air is aerosol-
blue and chill. I have notched
up your pitch-
pine scent and the maidenhair fern's
spry arousal.

[26]

And it would be just swell and dandy
to answer
them with my tonsure,
to return
with the black page from *Tristram Shandy*.

Yet the lichened
tree trunk will taper
to a point where one scrap of paper
is spiked, and my people yearn
for a legend:

*It may not be today
or tomorrow, but sooner or later
the Russians will water
their horses on the shores of Lough Erne
and Lough Neagh.*

Mink

A mink escaped from a mink-farm
in South Armagh
is led to the grave of Robert Nairac
by the fur-lined hood of his anorak. *garbot choice for IRA assassin*

undercover liason officer; tortured and killed by IRA

The Frog

Comes to mind as another small upheaval
amongst the rubble.
His eye matches exactly the bubble
in my spirit-level.
I set aside hammer and chisel
and take him on the trowel.

The entire population of Ireland
springs from a pair left to stand
overnight in a pond
in the gardens of Trinity College,
two bottles of wine left there to chill
after the Act of Union. *(1800 - made Ire. part of UK)*

There is, surely, in this story
a moral. A moral for our times. *▷ possibility for*
What if I put him to my head *servison*
and squeezed it out of him,
like the juice of freshly squeezed limes,
or a lemon sorbet?

*∨ myth that all frogs in Ire. come
from pair brought from France
on Champagne bottles - set in a
fountain to chill*

[29]

A Trifle

I had been meaning to work through lunch
the day before yesterday.
Our office block is the tallest in Belfast;
when the Tannoy sounds

another bomb alert
we take four or five minutes to run down
the thirty-odd flights of steps
to street level.

I had been trying to get past
a woman who held, at arm's length, a tray,
and on the tray the remains of her dessert—

a plate of blue-pink trifle
or jelly sponge,
with a dollop of whipped cream on top.

from Last Poems

IV

Not that I care who's sleeping with whom
now she's had her womb
removed, now it lies in its own glar
like the last beetroot in the pickle jar.

VII

I would have it, were I bold,
without relish, my own lightly broiled
heart on the side.

IX

I would be happy in the knowledge
that as I laboured up the no-through-road
towards your cottage
you ran to meet me. Your long white shift,
its spray of honesty and thrift.

XIV

Ours would be a worldly wisdom, heaven-sent;
the wisdom before the event.

Sky-Woman

When she hoiked it off
in the August dark

her blouse was man-made,
nylon or rayon.

I still see her under-
arm rash of sparks.

She has straddled me
since, like Orion.

More and more, I make
do with her umlaut

as, more and more, she
turns her back on me

to fumble with
the true Orion's belt.

Kissing and Telling

Or she would turn up *The Songs of Leonard Cohen*
on the rickety old gramophone.

And you knew by the way she unbound her tresses
and stepped from her William Morris dresses

you might just as well be anyone.

Goat's-milk cheeses, Navajo rugs,
her reading aloud from *A Dictionary of Drugs*—

she made wine of almost everything.

How many of those she found out on the street
and fetched back to her attic room—

to promise nothing, to take nothing for granted—

how many would hold by the axiom
she would intone as though it were her mantra?

I could name names. I could be indiscreet.

a passion w/o intimacy

The Unicorn Defends Himself

I

Somewhere in or around the turn
of the sixteenth century,
we come upon the fourth
in a series of Flemish tapestries
on the hunt of the unicorn.

Kicking out with his tattered hind
hooves, he tilts
at a hunting-hound
with his barley-sugar stick of horn;
the unicorn defends himself.

II

Once you swallowed a radar-blip
of peyote
you were out of your tree,
you hadn't a baldy
where you were or who you were with.

Only that you had fallen asleep
on the water bed
in a loft on the Lower East Side,
and woke between two bodies, true,
one wire-haired and one smooth.

The focal point is not, in truth,
his *coup de ventre*
to the milt-
sleek hunting-hound,
by which our eye is led astray.

Everything centres
on that spear tip poised to squander
the cleft
of his 'innocent behind'.
At Houston Street and Lafayette

the unicorn defends himself.

Blewits

They will be all fingers and thumbs
as they offer you a light
or try to catch the bar-tender's eye
for two fresh whiskey sours.

They will seem shy
as they help you with your wrap,
though their palms are spread
across your breasts. They hail a cab.

And later, in the wee, small hours,
you will lie on the bed
of your own entrails,

to be fist-fucked all night
by blewits, or by chanterelles,
until the morning that never comes.

N Unworthy imagery

The Destroying Angel

Will perch on your left epaulette
like a cockatoo
in her off-white ruff,
or the floosie traipsing through
the pavilion bar
in her mother's high-heeled shoes.
It is the eve of battle
and they—for now they are two—
they pout and preen themselves
and witter on about Nabokov.

Yes, lepidoptery.
So much more to him than *Lolita*.
So much. So very much.
They much prefer *A Russian Beauty*.
At last, one cockatoo flaps away
into the snow-dark sky
and one stays behind to smooch
in your left ear.
Another gin and Angostura bitters
and you are part of her dream

kitchen's ceramic hob,
the bathtub's
ever-deepening shades of avocado,
the various whatnots,
the row upon row of whodunnits . . .

The disembodied tinkle of a horse
outside your tent.
Otherwise all is calm.
The destroying angel wants to drink
to your campaign.
A gin and tonic, this time.
You will unbutton your tunic
and raise a glass. She raises hers.
Try as you may,
you cannot make them chink or chime.

Aisling

gaelic trad. of vision poetry

I was making my way home late one night
this summer, when I staggered
into a snow drift.

Her eyes spoke of a sloe-year,
her mouth a year of haws.

Was she Aurora, or the goddess Flora,
Artemidora, or Venus bright,
or Anorexia, who left
a lemon stain on my flannel sheet?

It's all much of a muchness.   — Irishism for "so what."

In Belfast's Royal Victoria Hospital
a kidney machine
supports the latest hunger-striker
to have called off his fast, a saline
drip into his bag of brine.

A lick and a promise. Cuckoo spittle.
I hand my sample to Doctor Maw.
She gives me back a confident *All Clear*.

[39]

The More a Man Has the More a Man Wants

At four in the morning he wakes
to the yawn of brakes,
the snore of a diesel engine.
Gone. All she left
is a froth of bra and panties.
The scum of the Seine
and the Farset.
Gallogly squats in his own pelt.
A sodium street light
has brought a new dimension
to their black taxi.
By the time they force an entry
he'll have skedaddled
among hen runs and pigeon lofts.

The charter flight from Florida
touched down at Aldergrove
minutes earlier,
at 3.54 a.m.
Its excess baggage takes the form
of Mangas Jones, Esquire,
who is, as it turns out, Apache.
He carries only hand luggage.
'Anything to declare?'
He opens the powder-blue attaché-
case. 'A pebble of quartz.'
'You're an Apache?' 'Mescalero.'
He follows the corridor's
arroyo till the signs read *Hertz*.

[40]

He is going to put his foot down
on a patch of waste ground
along the Stranmillis embankment
when he gets wind
of their impromptu fire.
The air above the once-sweet stream
is aquarium-
drained.
And six, maybe seven, skinheads
have formed a quorum
round a burnt-out heavy-duty tyre.
So intent on sniffing glue
they may not notice Gallogly,
or, if they do, are so far gone.

Three miles west as the crow flies
an all-night carry-out
provides the cover
for an illegal drinking club.
While the bar man unpacks a crate
of Coca-Cola,
one cool customer
takes on all comers in a video game.
He grasps what his two acolytes
have failed to seize.
Don't they know what kind of take-away
this is, the glipes?
Vietmanese. Viet-ma-friggin'-*knees*.
He drops his payload of napalm.

Gallogly is wearing a candy-stripe
king-size sheet,
a little something he picked up
off a clothes line.
He is driving a milk van
he borrowed from the Belfast Co-op
while the milkman's back
was turned.
He had given the milkman a playful
rabbit punch.
When he stepped on the gas
he flooded the street
with broken glass.
He is trying to keep a low profile.

The unmarked police car draws level
with his last address.
A sergeant and eight constables
pile out of a tender
and hammer up the stairs.
The street bristles with static.
Their sniffer dog, a Labrador bitch,
bursts into the attic
like David Balfour in *Kidnapped*.
A constable on his first dawn swoop
leans on a shovel.
He has turned over a
new leaf in her ladyship's herb patch.
They'll take it back for analysis.

All a bit much after the night shift
to meet a milkman
who's double-parked his van
closing your front door after him.
He's sporting your
Donegal tweed suit and your
Sunday shoes and politely raises your
hat as he goes by.
You stand there with your mouth open
as he climbs into the still-warm
driving seat of your Cortina
and screeches off towards the motorway,
leaving you uncertain
of your still-warm wife's damp tuft.

Someone on their way to early Mass
will find her hog-tied
to the chapel gates—
O Child of Prague—
big-eyed, anorexic.
The lesson for today
is pinned to her bomber jacket.
It seems to read *Keep off the Grass*.
Her lovely head has been chopped
and changed.
For Beatrice, whose fathers
knew Louis Quinze,
to have come to this, her perruque
of tar and feathers.

He is pushing the maroon Cortina
through the sedge
on the banks of the Callan.
It took him a mere forty minutes
to skite up the M1.
He followed the exit sign
for Loughgall and hared
among the top-heavy apple orchards.
This stretch of the Armagh/Tyrone
border was planted by Warwickshiremen
who planted in turn
their familiar quick-set damson hedges.
The Cortina goes to the bottom.
Gallogly swallows a plummy-plum-plum.

'I'll warrant them's the very pair
o' boys I seen abroad
in McParland's bottom, though where
in under God—
for thou art so possessed with murd'rous hate—
where they come from God only knows.'
'They were mad for a bite o' mate,
I s'pose.'
'I doubt so. I come across a brave dale
o' half-chawed damsels. Wanst wun disappeared
I follied the wun as yelly as Indy male.'
'Ye weren't afeared?'
'I follied him.' 'God save us.'
'An' he driv away in a van belongin' t'*Avis*.'

The grass sprightly as Astroturf
in the September frost
and a mist
here where the ground is low.
He seizes his own wrist
as if, as if
Blind Pew again seized Jim
at the sign of the 'Admiral Benbow'.
As if Jim Hawkins led Blind Pew
to Billy Bones
and they were all one and the same,
he stares in disbelief
at an Aspirin-white spot he pressed
into his own palm.

Gallogly's thorn-proof tweed jacket
is now several sizes too big.
He has flopped
down in a hay shed
to ram a wad of hay into the toe
of each of his ill-fitting
brogues, when he gets the drift
of ham and eggs.
Now he's led by his own wet nose
to the hacienda-style
farmhouse, a baggy-kneed animated
bear drawn out of the woods
by an apple pie
left to cool on a windowsill.

She was standing at the picture window
with a glass of water
and a Valium
when she caught your man
in the reflection of her face.
He came
shaping past the milking parlour
as if he owned the place.
Such is the integrity
of their quarrel
that she immediately took down
the legally held shotgun
and let him have both barrels.
She had wanted only to clear the air.

Half a mile away across the valley
her husband's U.D.R. patrol
is mounting a check-point.
He pricks up his ears
at the crack
of her prematurely arthritic hip-
joint,
and commandeers one of the jeeps.
There now, only a powder burn
as if her mascara had run.
The bloody puddle
in the yard, and the shilly-shally
of blood like a command wire
petering out behind a milk churn.

A hole in the heart, an ovarian
cyst.
Coming up the Bann
in a bubble.
Disappearing up his own bum.
Or, running on the spot
with all the minor aplomb
of a trick-cyclist.
So thin, side-on, you could spit
through him.
His six foot of pump water
bent double
in agony or laughter.
Keeping down-wind of everything.

White Annetts. Gillyflowers. Angel Bites.
When he names the forgotten names
of apples
he has them all off pat.
His eye like the eye of a travelling rat
lights on the studied negligence
of these scraws of turf.
A tarpaulin. A waterlogged pit.
He will take stock of the Kalashnikov's
filed-down serial number,
seven sticks of unstable
commercial gelignite
that have already begun to weep.
Red Strokes. Sugar Sweet. Widows Whelps.

Buy him a drink and he'll regale you
with how he came in for a cure
one morning after the night before
to the *Las Vegas* Lounge and Cabaret.
He was crossing the bar's
eternity of parquet floor
when his eagle eye
saw something move on the horizon.
If it wasn't an Indian.
A Sioux. An ugly Sioux.
He means, of course, an Oglala
Sioux busily tracing the family tree
of an Ulsterman who had some hand
in the massacre at Wounded Knee.

He will answer the hedge-sparrow's
Littlebitofbreadandnocheese
with a whole bunch
of freshly picked watercress,
a bulb of garlic,
sorrel,
with many-faceted blackberries.
Gallogly is out to lunch.
When his cock rattles its sabre
he takes it in his dab
hand, plants one chaste kiss
on its forelock,
and then, with a birl and a skirl,
tosses it off like a caber.

[48]

The U.D.R. corporal had come off duty
to be with his wife
while the others set about
a follow-up search.
When he tramped out just before twelve
to exercise the greyhound
he was hit by a single high-velocity
shot.
You could, if you like, put your fist
in the exit wound
in his chest.
He slumps
in the spume of his own arterial blood
like an overturned paraffin lamp.

Gallogly lies down in the sheugh
to munch
through a Beauty of
Bath. He repeats himself, *Bath*,
under his garlic-breath.
Sheugh, he says. *Sheugh*.
He is finding that first 'sh'
increasingly difficult to manage.
Sh-leeps. A milkmaid sinks
her bare foot
to the ankle
in a simmering dung hill
and fills the slot
with beastlings for him to drink.

[49]

In Ovid's conspicuously tongue-in-cheek
account of an eyeball
to eyeball
between the goddess Leto
and a shower of Lycian reed cutters
who refuse her a cup of cloudy
water
from their churned-up lake,
Live then forever in that lake of yours,
she cries, and has them
bubble
and squeak
and plonk themselves down as bullfrogs
in their icy jissom.

A country man kneels on his cap
beside his neighbour's fresh
grave-mud
as Gallogly kneels to lap
the primrose-yellow
custard.
The knees of his hand-me-down duds
are gingerish.
A pernickety seven-
year-old girl-child
parades in her mother's trousseau
and mumbles a primrose
Kleenex tissue
to make sure her lipstick's even.

Gallogly has only to part the veil
of its stomach wall
to get right under the skin,
the spluttering heart
and collapsed lung,
of the horse in *Guernica*.
He flees the Museum of Modern Art
with its bit between his teeth.
When he began to cough
blood, Hamsun rode the Minneapolis/
New York night train
on top of the dining-car.
One long, inward howl.
A porter-drinker without a thrapple.

A weekend trip to the mountains
North of Boston
with Alice, Alice A.
and her paprika hair,
the ignition key
to her family's Winnebago camper,
her quim
biting the leg off her.
In the oyster bar
of Grand Central Station
she gobbles a dozen Chesapeakes—
'Oh, I'm not particular as to size'—
and, with a flourish of tabasco,
turns to gobble him.

A brewery lorry on a routine delivery
is taking a slow,
dangerous bend.
The driver's blethering
his code name
over the Citizens' Band
when someone ambles
in front of him. Go, Johnny, Go, Go, Go.
He's been dry-gulched
by a sixteen-year-old numb
with Mogadon,
whose face is masked by the seamless
black stocking filched
from his mum.

When who should walk in but Beatrice,
large as life, or larger,
sipping her one glass of lager
and singing her one song.
If he had it to do all over again
he would let her shave his head
in memory of '98
and her own, the French, Revolution.
The son of the King of the Moy
met this child on the Roxborough
estate. *Noblesse*, she said. *Noblesse
oblige*. And her tiny nipples
were bruise-bluish, wild raspberries.
The song she sang was 'The Croppy Boy'.

Her *grand'mère* was once asked to tea
by Gertrude Stein,
and her *grand'mère* and Gertrude
and Alice B., *chère* Alice B.
with her hook-nose,
the three of them sat in the nude
round the petits fours
and repeated *Eros is Eros is Eros.*
If he had it to do all over again
he would still be taken in
by her Alice B. Toklas
Nameless Cookies
and those new words she had him learn:
hash, hashish, *lo perfido assassin.*

Once the local councillor straps
himself into the safety belt
of his Citroën
and skids up the ramp
from the municipal car park
he upsets the delicate balance
of a mercury-tilt
boobytrap.
Once they collect his smithereens
he doesn't quite add up.
They're shy of a foot, and a calf
which stems
from his left shoe like a severely
pruned-back shrub.

Ten years before. The smooth-as-a-
front-lawn at Queen's
where she squats
before a psilocybin god.
The indomitable gentle-bush
that had Lanyon or Lynn
revise their elegant ground plan
for the university quad.
With calmness, with care,
with breast milk, with dew.
There's no cure now.
There's nothing left to do.
The mushrooms speak through her.
Hush-hush.

'Oh, I'm not particular as to size,'
Alice hastily replied
and broke off a bit of the edge
with each hand
and set to work very carefully,
nibbling
first at one
and then the other.
On the Staten Island Ferry
two men are dickering
over the price
of a shipment of Armalites,
as Henry Thoreau was wont to quibble
with Ralph Waldo Emerson.

That last night in the Algonquin
he met with a flurry
of sprites,
the assorted shades
of Wolfe Tone, Napper Tandy,
a sanguine
Michael Cusack
brandishing his blackthorn.
Then, Thomas Meagher
darts up from the Missouri
on a ray
of the morning star
to fiercely ask
what has become of Irish hurling.

Everyone has heard the story of
a strong and beautiful bug
which came out of the dry leaf
of an old table of apple-tree wood
that stood
in a farmer's kitchen in Massachusetts
and which was heard gnawing out
for several weeks—
When the phone trills
he is careful not to lose his page—
Who knows what beautiful and winged life
whose egg
has been buried for ages
may unexpectedly come forth? 'Tell-tale.'

Gallogly carries a hunting bow
equipped
with a bow sight
and a quiver
of hunting arrows
belonging to her brother.
Alice has gone a little way off
to do her job.
A timber wolf,
a caribou,
or merely a trick of the light?
As, listlessly,
he lobs
an arrow into the undergrowth.

Had you followed the river Callan's
Pelorus Jack
through the worst drought
in living memory
to the rains of early Autumn
when it scrubs its swollen,
scab-encrusted back
under a bridge, the bridge you look down from,
you would be unlikely to pay much heed
to yet another old banger
no one could be bothered to tax,
or a beat-up fridge
well-stocked with gelignite,
or some five hundred yards of Cortex.

He lopes after the dribs of blood
through the pine forest
till they stop dead
in the ruins of a longhouse
or hogan.
Somehow, he finds his way
back to their tent.
Not so much as a whiff of her musk.
The girl behind the Aer Lingus
check-in desk
at Logan
is wearing the same scent
and an embroidered capital letter *A*
on her breast.

Was she Aurora, or the goddess Flora,
Artemidora, or Venus bright,
or Helen fair beyond compare
That Priam stole from the Grecian sight?
Quite modestly she answered me
and she gave her head one fetch up
and she said I am gathering musheroons
to make my mammy ketchup.
The dunt and dunder
of a culvert-bomb
wakes him
as it might have woke Leander.
And she said I am gathering musheroons
to make my mammy ketchup O.

Predictable as the gift of the gab
or a drop of the craythur
he noses round the six foot deep
crater.
Oblivious to their Landrover's
olive-drab
and the Burgundy berets
of a snatch-squad of Paratroopers.
Gallogly, or Gollogly,
otherwise known as Golightly,
otherwise known as Ingoldsby,
otherwise known as English,
gives forth one low cry of anguish
and agrees to come quietly.

They have bundled him into the cell
for a strip-
search.
He perches
on the balls of his toes, my my,
with his legs spread
till both his instep arches
fall.
He holds himself at arm's
length from the brilliantly Snowcem-ed
wall, a game bird
hung by its pinion tips
till it drops, in the fullness of time,
from the mast its colours are nailed to.

They have left him to cool his heels
after the obligatory
bath,
the mug shots, fingerprints
et cetera.
He plumps the thin bolster
and hints
at the slop bucket.
Six o'clock.
From the A Wing of Armagh jail
he can make out
the Angelus bell
of St Patrick's cathedral
and a chorus of 'For God and Ulster'.

The brewery lorry's stood at a list
by the *Las Vegas*
throughout the afternoon,
its off-side rear tyres down.
As yet, no one has looked agog
at the smuts and rusts
of a girlie mag
in disarray on the passenger seat.
An almost invisible, taut
fishing line
runs from the Playmate's navel
to a pivotal
beer keg.
As yet, no one has risen to the bait.

unspoken connection between sex and violence

I saw no mountains, no enormous spaces,
no magical growth and metamorphosis
of buildings, nothing remotely like
a drama or a parable
in which he dons these lime-green
dungarees,
green Wellingtons,
a green helmet of aspect terrible.
The other world to which mescalin
admitted me was not the world of visions;
it existed out there, in what I could see
with my eyes open.
He straps a chemical pack on his back
and goes in search of some Gawain.

Gallogly pads along the block
to raise his visor
at the first peep-hole.
He shamelessly
takes in her lean piglet's
back, the back
and boyish hams
of a girl at stool.
At last. A tiny goat's-pill.
A stub of crayon
with which she has squiggled
a shamrock, yes,
but a shamrock after the school
of Pollock, Jackson Pollock.

I stopped and stared at her face to face
and on the spot a name came to me,
a name with a smooth, nervous sound:
Ylayali.
When she was very close
I drew myself up straight
and said in an impressive voice,
'Miss, you are losing your book.'
And Beatrice, for it is she, she squints
through the spy-hole
to pass him an orange,
an Outspan orange some visitor has spiked
with a syringe-ful
of vodka.

The more a man has the more a man wants,
the same I don't think true.
For I never met a man with one black eye
who ever wanted two.
In the *Las Vegas* Lounge and Cabaret
the resident group—
pot bellies, Aran knits—
have you eating out of their hands.
Never throw a brick at a drowning man
when you're near to a grocer's store.
Just throw him a cake of Sunlight soap,
let him wash himself ashore.
You will act the galoot, and gallivant,
and call for another encore.

Gallogly, Gallogly, O Gallogly
juggles
his name like an orange
between his outsize baseball glove
paws,
and ogles
a moon that's just out of range
beyond the perimeter wall.
He works a gobbet of Brylcreem
into his quiff
and delves
through sand and gravel,
shrugging it off
his velveteen shoulders and arms.

Just
throw
him
a
cake
of
Sunlight
soap,
let
him
wash
him-
self
ashore.

Into a picture by Edward Hopper
of a gas station
in the mid-West
where Hopper takes as his theme
light, the spooky
glow of an illuminated sign
reading Esso or Mobil
or what-have-you—
into such a desolate oval
ride two youths on a motorbike.
A hand gun. Balaclavas.
The pump attendant's grown so used
to hold-ups he calls after them:
Beannacht Dé ar an obair. — garlic
God bless you in
your work

The pump attendant's not to know
he's being watched by a gallowglass
hot-foot from a woodcut
by Derricke,
who skips across the forecourt
and kicks the black
plastic bucket
they left as a memento.
Nor is the gallowglass any the wiser.
The bucket's packed with fertilizer
and a heady brew
of sugar and Paraquat's
relentlessly gnawing its way through
the floppy knot of a Durex.

[63]

It was this self-same pump attendant
who dragged the head and torso
clear
and mouthed an Act of Contrition
in the frazzled ear
and overheard
those already-famous last words
Moose . . . Indian.
'Next of all wus the han'.' 'Be Japers.'
'The sodgers cordonned-off the area
wi' what-ye-may-call-it tape.'
'Lunimous.' 'They foun' this hairy
han' wi' a drowneded man's grip
on a lunimous stone no bigger than a . . .'

'Huh.'

quotation from Robert Frost